The Alchemical Catechism of Paracelsus

By
Paracelsus

Copyright © 2021 Lamp of Trismegistus. All rights reserved. No part of this publication may be reproduced or transmitted in any form or by any means, electronic or mechanical, including photocopying, recording, or by any information storage and retrieval system, without permission in writing from Lamp of Trismegistus. Reviewers may quote brief passages.

ISBN: 978-1-63118-513-7

Esoteric Classics

Other Books in this Series and Related Titles

Aurora of the Philosophers by Paracelsus (978-1-63118-507-6)

The Stone of the Philosophers by A E Waite (978-1-63118-509-0)

The Magician's Heavenly Chaos by Thomas Vaughan (978-1-63118-500-7)

On the Philadelphian Gold by Philochrysus & Philadelphus (978-1-63118-511-3)

Paracelsus, the Four Elements and Their Spirits by M P Hall (978-1-63118-400-0)

Alchemy in the Nineteenth Century by Helena P. Blavatsky (978-1-63118-446-8)

Cloud Upon the Sanctuary by Waite & K Eckartshausen (978-1-63118-438-3)

The Rosicrucian Chemical Marriage by Christian Rosenkreuz (978-1-63118-458-1)

The Golden Verses of Pythagoras: Five Translations (978-1-63118-479-6)

The Hymns of Hermes by G. R. S. Mead (978-1-63118-405-5)

The Devil in Love by Jacques Cazotte (978–1–63118–499–4)

On the Cave of the Nymphs in the Odyssey by Thomas Taylor (978-1-63118-505-2)

Plato and Platonism and Related Esoteric Essays by various (978-1-63118-432-1)

Clairvoyance and Psychic Abilities by A Besant &c (978-1-63118-403-1)

The Book of Wisdom of Solomon by King Solomon (978-1-63118-502-1)

A Collection of Early Writings on Astral Travel (978-1-63118-477-2)

Rosicrucian Rules, Secret Signs, Codes and Symbols by various (978-1-63118-488-8)

The Sepher Yetzirah and the Qabalah by M P Hall (978-1-63118-481-9)

Arcane Formulas or Mental Alchemy by W W Atkinson (978-1-63118-459-8)

The Machinery of the Mind by Dion Fortune (978-1-63118-451-2)

The Leadbeater Reader: A Selection of Occult Essays (978-1-63118-483-3)

Audio versions are also available on Audible, Amazon and Apple

Other Books in this Series and Related Titles

Atlantis, the Gods of Antiquity and the Myth of the Dying God (978–1–63118–498–7)

The Mysteries of Freemasonry & the Druids by M P Hall &c (978-1-63118-444-4)

Prashna Upanishad and Commentary by Charles Johnston (978-1-63118-494-9)

The Kabbalah of Masonry & Related Writings by E Levi &c (978-1-63118-453-6)

A Collection of Fiction and Essays by Occult Writers on Supernatural and Metaphysical Subjects by various (978–1–63118–510–6)

The First and Second Gospels of the Infancy of Jesus Christ by Thomas and James (978-1-63118-415-4)

The Secrets of Enoch by Enoch (978-1-63118-449-9)

Brothers & Builders by Joseph Fort Newton (978-1-63118-506-9)

Magical Essays and Instructions by Florence Farr (978-1-63118-418-5)

Masonic and Rosicrucian History by M P Hall & H Voorhis (978-1-63118-486-4)

History and Teachings of the Rosicrucians by W W Westcott &c (978-1-63118-487-1)

The Smoky God or A Voyage to the Inner World by Emerson (978-1-63118-423-9)

The Janeites, The Man Who Would Be King and Other Stories of Freemasonry by Rudyard Kipling (978–1–63118–480–2)

Gnosis of the Mind by G. R. S. Mead (978-1-63118-408-6)

The Life of Pythagoras by Porphyry (978-1-63118-512-0)

The Influence of Pythagoras on Freemasonry and Other Essays (978-1-63118-404-8)

The Master Mason's Handbook by J S M Ward (978-1-63118-474-1)

The Feminine Occult by various authors (978-1-63118-711-7)

The Path of Light: A Manual of Maha-Yana Buddhism (978-1-63118-471-0)

The Sword of Welleran and Other Stories by Lord Dunsany (978-1-63118-501-4)

Audio versions are also available on Audible, Amazon and Apple

Table of Contents

Introduction

Page 7

A Short Catechism of Alchemy

Page 9

INTRODUCTION

The word "esoteric" can be difficult to define. Esotericism in general can be seen less as a system of beliefs and more as a category, which encompasses numerous, different systems of beliefs. It's a bit of juxtaposition, since the word "esoteric" indicates something that few people know about, while the term itself broadly covers numerous philosophies, practices, areas of study and belief systems.

In a greater sense, Esotericism acts as a storehouse for secret knowledge, which is often considered ancient (*by tradition, if not by fact*), passed down from generation to generation, in private. At various times in history, simply possessing the knowledge of some of these subjects, was considered illegal and a jailable offence, if discovered. This usually included such general topics as Alchemy, Pharmacology, Qabalah, Hermeticism, Occultism, Ceremonial Magic, Astrology, Divination, Rosicrucianism and so on. Collectively, these areas of study were often referred to as the esoteric sciences.

Sometimes, the outer garment of a subject isn't esoteric, while what is hidden beneath it, is. As an example, Freemasonry isn't necessarily esoteric by nature (at *least not anymore*), but certain signs, passwords and handshakes given to the candidate during their initiation, are in fact, esoteric, in the sense that they are hidden from the general public.

Today, in the twenty-first century, such topics are readily available at bookstores across the country, and numerous mainsteam publishers offer beginners guides and coffee-table volumes on many of these subjects, intended for mass appeal. Books like *"The Secret"* have turned previously arcane topics into household knowledge. All that being the case, however, it isn't to say that there still aren't buried secrets to uncover, ancient wisdom being ignored and forgotten mysteries to be explored. In fact, it is often that we are only able to further our own studies by standing on the shoulders of these disappearing giants.

Lamp of Trismegistus is doing its part to help preserve humanity's esoteric history by making some of these classics available to those students who are seeking to unearth the knowledge of these ancient colossi.

So, be sure to check other titles from our *Esoteric Classics* series, as well as our *Occult Fiction, Theosophical Classics, Foundations of Freemasonry Series, Supernatural Fiction, Paranormal Research Series, Studies in Buddhism* and our *Christian Apocrypha Series*. You can also download the audio versions of most of these titles from Amazon, Apple or Audible, for learning on the go.

A SHORT CATECHISM OF ALCHEMY

Q. What is the chief study of a Philosopher?
A. It is the investigation of the operations of Nature.

Q. What is the end of Nature?
A. God, Who is also its beginning.

Q. Whence are all things derived?
A. From one and indivisible Nature.

Q. Into how many regions is Nature separated?
A. Into four palmary regions.

Q. Which are they?
A. The dry, the moist, the warm, and the cold, which are the four elementary qualities, whence all things originate.

Q. How is Nature differentiated?
A. Into male and female.

Q. To what may we compare Nature?
A. To Mercury.

Q. Give a concise definition of Nature.
A. It is not visible, though it operates visibly; for it is simply a volatile spirit, fulfilling its office in bodies, and animated by the universal spirit-the divine breath, the central and universal fire, which vivifies all things that exist.

Q. What should be the qualities possessed by the examiners of Nature?

A. They should be like unto Nature herself. That is to say, they should be truthful, simple, patient, and persevering.

Q. What matters should subsequently engross their attention?
A. The philosophers should most carefully ascertain whether their designs are in harmony with Nature, and of a possible and attainable kind; if they would accomplish by their own power anything that is usually performed by the power of Nature, they must imitate her in every detail.

Q. What method must be followed in order to produce something which shall be developed to a superior degree than Nature herself develops it.
A. The manner of its improvement must be studied, and this is invariably operated by means of a like nature. For example, if it be desired to develop the intrinsic virtue of a given metal beyond its natural condition, the chemist must avail himself of the metallic nature itself, and must be able to discriminate between its male and female differentiations.

Q. Where does the metallic nature store her seeds?
A. In the four elements.

Q. With what materials can the philosopher alone accomplish anything?
A. With the germ of the given matter; this is its elixir or quintessence, more precious by far, and more useful, to the artist, than is Nature herself. Before the philosopher has extracted the seed, or germ, Nature, in his behalf, will be ready to perform her duty.

Q. What is the germ, or seed, of any substance?
A. It is the most subtle and perfect decoction and digestion of the substance itself; or, rather, it is the Balm of Sulphur, which is identical with the Radical Moisture of Metals.

Q. By what is this seed, or germ, engendered?
A. By the four elements, subject to the will of the Supreme Being, and through the direct intervention of the imagination of Nature.

Q. After what manner do the four elements operate?
A. By means of an incessant and uniform motion, each one, according to its quality, depositing its seed in the centre of the earth, where it is subjected to action and digested, and is subsequently expelled in an outward direction by the laws of movement.

Q. What do the philosophers understand by the centre of the earth?
A. A certain void place where nothing may repose, and the existence of which is assumed.

Q. Where, then, do the four elements expel and deposit their seeds?
A. In the ex-centre, or in the margin and circumference of the centre, which, after it has appropriated a portion, casts out the surplus into the region of excrement, scoriae, fire, and formless chaos.

Q. Illustrate this teaching by an example.
A. Take any level table, and set in its centre a vase filled with water; surround the vase with several things of various

colours, especially salt, taking care that a proper distance intervenes between them all. Then pour out the water from the vase, and it will flow in streams here and there; one will encounter a substance of a red colour, and will assume a tinge of red; another will pass over the salt, and will contract a saline flavour; for it is certain that water does not modify the places which it traverses, but the diverse characteristics of places change the nature of water. In the same way the seed which is deposited by the four elements at the centre of the earth is subject to a variety of modifications in the places through which it passes, so that every existing substance is produced in the likeness of its channel, and when a seed on its arrival at a certain point encounters pure earth and pure water, a pure substance results, but the contrary in an opposite case.

Q. After what manner do the elements procreate this seed?
A. In order to the complete elucidation of this point, it must be observed that there are two gross and heavy elements and two that are volatile in character. Two, in like manner, are dry and two humid, one out of the four being actually excessively dry, and the other excessively moist. They are also masculine and feminine. Now, each of them has a marked tendency to reproduce its own species within its own sphere. Moreover, they are never in repose, but are perpetually interacting, and each of them separates, of and by itself, the most subtle portion thereof. Their general place of meeting is in the centre, even the centre of the Archeus, that servant of Nature, where coming to mix their several seeds, they agitate and finally expel them to the exterior.

Q. What is the true and the first matter of all metals?
A. The first matter, properly so called, is dual in its essence, or is in itself of a twofold nature; one, nevertheless, cannot create a metal without the concurrence of the other. The first and the palmary essence is an aerial humidity, blended with a warm air, in the form of a fatty water, which adheres to all substances indiscriminately, whether they are pure or impure.

Q. How has this humidity been named by Philosophers?
A. Mercury.

Q. By what is it governed?
A. By the rays of the Sun and Moon.

Q. What is the second matter?
A. The warmth of the earth -otherwise, that dry heat which is termed Sulphur by the Philosophers.

Q. Can the entire material body be converted into seed?
A. Its eight-hundredth part only-that, namely, which is secreted in the centre of the body in question, and may, for example, be seen in a grain of wheat.

Q. Of what use is the bulk of the matter as regards its seed?
A. It is useful as a safeguard against excessive heat, cold, moisture, or aridity, and, in general, all hurtful inclemency, against which it acts as an envelope.

Q. Would those artists who pretend to reduce the whole matter of any body into seed derive any advantage from the process, supposing it were possible to perform it?
A. None; on the contrary, their labour would be wholly

unproductive, because nothing that is good can be accomplished by a deviation from natural methods.

Q. What, therefore, should be done?
A. The matter must be effectively separated from its impurities, for there is no metal, how pure soever, which is entirely free from imperfections, though their extent varies. Now all superfluities, cortices, and scoriae must be peeled off and purged out from the matter in order to discover its seed.

Q. What should receive the most careful attention of the Philosopher?
A. Assuredly, the end of Nature, and this is by no means to be looked for in the vulgar metals, because, these having issued already from the hands of the fashioner, it is no longer to be found therein.

Q. For what precise reason?
A. Because the vulgar metals, and chiefly gold, are absolutely dead, while ours, on the contrary, are absolutely living, and possess a soul.

Q. What is the life of metals?
A. It is no other substance than fire, when they are as yet imbedded in the mines.

Q. What is their death?
A. Their life and death are in reality one principle, for they die, as they live, by fire, but their death is from a fire of fusion.

Q. After what manner are metals conceived in the womb of the earth?
A. When the four elements have developed their power or

virtue in the centre of the earth, and have deposited their seed, the Archeus of Nature, in the course of a distillatory process, sublimes them superficially by the warmth and energy of the perpetual movement.

Q. Into what does the wind resolve itself when it is distilled through the pores of the earth?
A. It resolves itself into water, whence all things spring; in this state it is merely a humid vapour, out of which there is subsequently evolved the principiated principle of all substances, which also serves as the first matter of the Philosophers.

Q. What then is this principiated principle, which is made use of as the first matter by the Children of Knowledge in the philosophic achievement?
A. It is this identical matter, which, the moment it is conceived, receives a permanent and unchangeable form.

Q. Are Saturn, Jupiter, Mars, Venus, the Sun, the Moon, etc., separately endowed with individual seed?
A. One is common to them all; their differences are to be accounted for by the: locality from which they are derived, not to speak of the fact that Nature completes her work with far greater rapidity in the procreation of silver than in that of gold, and so of the other metals, each in its own proportion.

Q. How is gold formed in the bowels of the earth?
A. When this vapour, of which we have spoken, is sublimed in the centre of the earth, and when it has passed through warm and pure places, where a certain sulphureous grease adheres to the channels, then this vapour, which the

Philosophers have denominated their Mercury, becomes adapted and joined to this grease, which it sublimes with itself; from such amalgamation there is produced a certain unctuousness, which, abandoning the vaporous form, assumes that of grease, and is sublimised in other places, which have been cleansed by this preceding vapour, and the earth whereof has consequently been rendered more subtle, pure, and humid; it fills the pores of this earth, is joined thereto, and gold is produced as a result.

Q. How is Saturn engendered?
A. It occurs when the said unctuosity, or grease, passes through places which are totally impure and cold.

Q. How is Venus brought forth?
A. She is produced in localities where the earth itself is pure, but is mingled with impure sulphur.

Q. What power does the vapour, which we have recently mentioned, possess in the centre of the earth?
A. By its continual progress it has the power of perpetually rarefying whatsoever is crude and impure, and of successively attracting to itself all that is pure around it.

Q. What is the seed of the first matter of all things?
A. The first matter of things, that is to say, the matter of principiating principles is begotten by Nature, without the assistance of any other seed; in other words, Nature receives the matter from the elements, whence it subsequently brings forth the seed.

Q. What, absolutely speaking, is therefore the seed of things?
A. The seed in a body is no other thing than a congealed air, or a humid vapour, which is useless except it be dissolved by a warm vapour.

Q. How is the generation of seed comprised in the metallic kingdom?
A. By the artifice of Archeus the four elements, in the first generation of Nature, distil a ponderous vapour of water into the centre of the earth ; this is the seed of metals, and it is called Mercury, not on account of its essence, but because of its fluidity, and the facility with which it will adhere to each and every thing.

Q. Why is this vapour compared to sulphur?
A. Because of its internal heat.

Q. From what species of Mercury are we to conclude that the metals are composed?
A. The reference is exclusively to the Mercury of the Philosophers, and in no sense to the common or vulgar substance, which cannot become a seed, seeing that, like other metals, it already contains its own seed.

Q. What, therefore, must actually be accepted as the subject of our matter?
A. The seed alone, otherwise the fixed grain, and not the whole body, which is differentiated into Sulphur, or living male, and into Mercury, or living female.

Q. What operation must be afterwards performed
A. They must be joined together, so that they may form a

germ, after which they will proceed to the procreation of a fruit which is conformed to their nature.

Q. What is the part of the artist in this operation?
A. The artist must do nothing but separate that which is subtle from that which is gross.

Q. To what, therefore, is the whole philosophic combination reduced?
A. The development of one into two, and the reduction of two into one, and nothing further.

Q. Whither must we turn for the seed and life of meals and minerals?
A. The seed of minerals is properly the water which exists in the centre
And the heart of the minerals.

Q. How does Nature operate by the help of Art?
A. Every seed, whatsoever its kind, is useless, unless by Nature or Art it is placed in a suitable matrix, where it receives its life by the coction of the germ! and by the congelation of the pure particle, or fixed grain.

Q. How is the seed subsequently nourished and preserved?
A. By the warmth of its body.

Q. What is therefore performed by the artist in the mineral kingdom?
A. He finishes what cannot be finished by Nature on account of the crudity of the air, which has permeated the pores of all bodies by its violence, but on the surface and not in the bowels of the earth.

Q. What correspondence have the metals among themselves?
A. It is necessary for a proper comprehension of the nature of this correspondence to consider the position of the planets, and to pay attention to Saturn, which is the highest of all, and then is succeeded by Jupiter, next by Mars, the Sun, Venus, Mercury, and, lastly, by the Moon. It must be observed that the influential virtues of the planets do not ascend but descend, and experience teaches us that Mars can be easily converted into Venus, not Venus into Mars, which is of a lower sphere. So, also, Jupiter can be easily transmuted into Mercury, because Jupiter is superior to Mercury, the one being second after the firmament, the other second above the earth, and Saturn is highest of all, while the Moon is lowest. The Sun enters into all, but it is never ameliorated by its inferiors. It is clear that there is a large correspondence between Saturn and the Moon, in the middle of which is the Sun; but to all these changes the Philosopher should strive to administer the Sun.

Q. When the Philosophers speak of gold and silver, from which they extract their matter, are we to suppose that they refer to the vulgar gold and silver?
A. By no means; vulgar silver and gold are dead, while those of the Philosophers are full of life.

Q. What is the object of research among the Philosophers?
A. Proficiency in the art of perfecting what Nature has left imperfect in the mineral kingdom, and the attainment of the treasure of the Philosophical Stone.

Q. What is this Stone?
A. The Stone is nothing else than the radical humidity of the

elements, perfectly purified and educed into a sovereign fixation, which causes it to perform such great things for health, life being resident exclusively in the humid radical.

Q. In what does the secret of accomplishing this admirable work consist?
A. It consists in knowing how to educe from potentiality into activity the innate warmth, or the fire of Nature, which is enclosed in the centre of the radical humidity.

Q. What are the precautions which must be made use of to guard against failure in the work?
A. Great pains must be taken to eliminate excrements from the matter, and to conserve nothing but the kernel, which contains all the virtue of the compound.

Q. Why does this medicine heal every species of disease?
A. It is not on account of tile variety of its qualities, but simply because it powerfully fortifies the natural warmth, which it gently stimulates, while other physics irritate it by too violent an action.

Q How can you demonstrate to me the truth of the art in the matter of the tincture?
A. Firstly, its truth is founded on the fact that the physical powder, being composed of the same substance as the metals, namely, quicksilver, has the faculty of combining with these in fusion, one nature easily embracing another which is like itself. Secondly, seeing that the imperfection of the base metals is owing to the crudeness of their quicksilver, and to that alone, the physical powder, which is a ripe and decocted quicksilver, and, in itself a pure fire, can easily communicate

to them its own maturity, and can transmute them into its nature, after it has attracted their crude humidity, that is to say, their quicksilver, which is the sole substance that transmutes them, the rest being nothing but scoriae and excrements, which are rejected in projection.

Q. What road should the Philosopher follow that he may attain to the knowledge and execution of the physical work?
A. That precisely which was followed by the Great Architect of the Universe in the creation of the world, by observing how the chaos was evolved.

Q. What was the matter of the chaos?
A. It could be nothing else than a humid vapour, because water alone enters into all created substances, which all finish in a strange term, this term being a proper subject for the impression of all forms.

Q. Give me an example to illustrate what you have just stated.
A. An example may be found in the special productions of composite substances, the seeds of which invariably begin by resolving themselves into a certain humour, which is the chaos of the particular matter, whence issues, by a kind of irradiation, the complete form of the plant. Moreover, it should be observed that Holy Scripture makes no mention of anything except water as the material subject whereupon the Spirit of God brooded, nor of anything except light as the universal form of things.

Q. What profit may the Philosopher derive from these considerations, and what should he especially remark in the method of creation which was pursued by the Supreme

Being?

A. In the first place he should observe the matter out of which the world was made; he will see that out of this confused mass, the Sovereign Artist began by extracting light, that this light in the same moment dissolved the darkness which covered the face of the earth, and that it served as the universal form of the matter. He will then easily perceive that in the generation of all composite substances, a species of irradiation takes place, and a separation of light and darkness, wherein Nature is an undeviating copyist of her Creator. The Philosopher will equally understand after what manner, by the action of this light, the empyrean, or firmament which divides the superior and inferior waters, was subsequently produced; how the sky was studded with luminous bodies; and how the necessity for the moon arose, which was owing to the space intervening between the things above and the things below; for the moon is an intermediate torch between the superior and the inferior worlds, receiving the celestial influences and communicating them to the earth. Finally he will understand how the Creator, in the gathering of the waters, produced dry land.

Q. How many heavens can you enumerate?
A. Properly there is one only, which is the firmament that divides the waters from the waters. Nevertheless, three are admitted, of which the first is the space that is above the clouds. In this heaven the waters are rarefied, and fall upon the fixed stars, and it is also in this space that the planets and wandering stars perform their revolutions. The second heaven

is the firmament of the fixed stars, while the third is the abode of the supercelestial waters.

Q. Why is the rarefaction of the waters confined to the first heaven?
A. Because it is in the nature of rarefied substances to ascend, and because God, in His eternal laws, has assigned its proper sphere to everything.

Q. Why does each celestial body invariably revolve about an axis?
A. It is by reason of the primeval impetus which it received, and by virtue of the same law which will cause any heavy substance suspended from a thread to turn with the same velocity, if the power which impels its motion be always equal.

Q. Why do the superior waters never descend?
A. Because of their extreme rarefaction. It is for this reason that a skilled chemist can derive more profit from the study of rarefaction than from any other science whatsoever.

Q. What is the matter of the firmament?
A. It is properly air, which is more suitable than water as a medium of light.

Q. After the separation of the waters from the dry earth, what was performed by the Creator to originate generation?
A. He created a certain light which was destined for this office; He placed it in the central fire, and moderated this fire by the humidity of water and by the coldness of earth, so as to keep a check upon its energy and adapt it to His design.

Q. What is the action of this central fire?
A. It continually operates upon the nearest humid matter, which it exalts into vapour; now this vapour is the mercury of Nature and the first matter of the three kingdoms.

Q. How is the sulphur of Nature subsequently formed?
A. By the interaction of the central fire and the mercurial vapour.

Q. How is the salt of the sea produced?
A. By the action of the same fire upon aqueous humidity, when the aerial humidity, which is contained therein, has been exhaled.

Q. What should be done by a truly wise Philosopher when he has once mastered the foundation and the order in the procedure of the Great Architect of the Universe in the construction of all that exists in Nature?
A. He should, as far as may be possible, become a faithful copyist of his Creator. In the physical chaos he should make his chaos such as the original actually was; he should separate the light from the darkness : he should form his firmament for the separation of the waters which are above from the waters which are below, and should successively accomplish, point by point, the entire sequence of the creative act.

Q. With what is this grand and sublime operation performed?
A. With one single corpuscle, or minute body, which, so to speak, contains nothing but faeces, filth, and abominations, but whence a certain tenebrous and mercurial humidity is extracted, which contains in itself all that is required by the

Philosopher, because, as a fact, he is in search of nothing hut the true Mercury.

Q. What kind of mercury, therefore, must he make use of in performing the work?
A. Of a mercury which, as such, is not found on the earth, but is extracted from bodies, yet not from vulgar mercury, as it has been falsely said.

Q. Why is the latter unfitted to the needs of our work?
A. Because the wise artist must take notice that vulgar mercury has an insufficient quantity of sulphur, and he should consequently operate upon a body created by Nature, in which Nature herself has united the sulphur and mercury that it is the work of the artist to separate.

Q. What must he subsequently do?
A. He must purify them and join them anew together.

Q. How do you denominate the body of which we have been speaking?
A. The RUDE STONE, Or Chaos, or Iliaste, or Hyle--that confused mass which is known but universally despised.

Q. As you have told me that Mercury is the one thing which the Philosopher must absolutely understand, will you give me a circumstantial description of it, so as to avoid misconception?
A. In respect of its nature, our Mercury is dual--fixed and volatile; in regard to its motion, it is also dual, for it has a motion of ascent and of descent; by that of descent, it is the influence of plants, by which it stimulates the drooping fire of Nature, and this is its first office previous to congelation. By

its ascensional movement, it rises, seeking to be purified, and as this is after congelation, it is considered to be the radical moisture of substances, which, beneath its vile scoriae, still preserves the nobility of its first origin.

Q. How many species of moisture do you suppose to be in each composite thing?
A. There are three--the Elementary, which is properly the vase of the other elements; the Radical, which, accurately speaking, is the oil, or balm, in which the entire virtue of the subject is resident--lastly, the Alimentary, the true natural dissolvent, which draws up the drooping internal fire, causing corruption and blackness by its humidity, and fostering and sustaining the subject.

Q. How many species of Mercury are there known to the Philosophers?
A. The Mercury of the Philosophers may be regarded under four aspects; the first is entitled the Mercury of bodies, which is actually their concealed seed; the second is the Mercury of Nature, which is the Bath or Vase of the Philosophers, otherwise the humid radical; to the third has been applied the designation, Mercury of the Philosophers, because it is found in their laboratory and in their minera. It is the sphere of Saturn; it is the Diana of the Wise; it is the true salt of metals, after the acquisition of which the true philosophic work may be truly said to have begun. In its fourth aspect, it is called Common Mercury, which yet is not that of the Vulgar, but rather is properly the true air of the Philosophers, the true middle substance of water, the true secret and concealed fire, called also common fire, because it is common to all minerae,

for it is the substance of metals, and thence do they derive their quantity and quality.

Q. How many operations art comprised in our work?
A. There is one only, which may be resolved into sublimation, and sublimation, according to Geber, is nothing other than the elevation of the dry matter by the mediation of fire, with adherence to its own vase.

Q. What precaution should be taken in reading the Hermetic Philosophers?
A. Great care, above all, must be observed upon this point, lest what they say upon the subject should be interpreted literally and in accordance with the mere sound of the words: For the letter killeth, but the spirit giveth life.

Q. What books should be read in order to have an acquaintance with our science?
A. Among the ancients, all the works of Hermes should especially be studied; in the next place, a certain book, entitled The Passage of the Red Sea, and another, The Entrance into the Promised Land. Paracelsus also should be read before all among elder writers, and, among other treatises, his Chemical Pathway, or the Manual of Paracelsus, which contains all the mysteries of demonstrative physics and the most arcane Kabbalah. This rare and unique manuscript work exists only in the Vatican Library, but Sendivogius had the good fortune to take a copy of it, which has helped in the illumination of the sages of our order. Secondly, Raymond Lully must be read, and his Vade Mecum above all, his dialogue called the Tree of Life, his testament, and his codicil. There must,

however, be a certain precaution exercised in respect to the two last, because, like those of Geber, and also of Arnold de Villanova, they abound in false recipes and futile fictions, which seem to have been inserted with the object of more effectually disguising the truth from the ignorant. In the third place, the Turba Philosophorum which is a collection of ancient authors, contains much that is materially good, though there is much also which is valueless. Among mediaeval writers Zachary, Trevisan, Roger Bacon, and a certain anonymous author, whose book is entitled The Philosophers, should be held especially high in the estimation of the student. Among moderns the most worthy to be prized are John Fabricius, Francois de Nation, and Jean D'Espagnet, who wrote Physics Restored, though, to say the truth, he has imported some false precepts and fallacious opinions into his treatise.

Q. When may the Philosopher venture to undertake the work?
A. When he is, theoretically, able to extract, by means of a crude spirit, a digested spirit out of a body in dissolution, which digested spirit he must again rejoin to the vital oil.

Q. Explain me this theory in a clearer manner.
A. It may be demonstrated more completely in the actual process; the great experiment may be undertaken when the Philosopher, by the medium of a vegetable menstruum, united to a mineral menstruum, is qualified to dissolve a third essential menstruum, with which menstruums united he must wash the earth, and then exalt it into a celestial quintessence, to compose the sulphureous thunderbolt, which

instantaneously penetrates substances and destroys their excrements.

Q. Have those persons a proper acquaintance with Nature who pretend to make use of vulgar gold for seed, and of vulgar mercury for the dissolvent, or the earth in which it should be sown?
A. Assuredly not, because neither the one nor the other possesses the external agent--gold, because it has been deprived of it by decoction, and mercury because it has never had it.

Q. In seeking this auriferous seed elsewhere than in gold itself, is there no danger of producing a species of monster, since one appears to be departing from Nature?
A. It is undoubtedly true that in gold is contained the auriferous seed, and that in a more perfect condition than it is found in any other body; but this does not force us to make use of vulgar gold, for such a seed is equally found in each of the other metals, and is nothing else but that fixed grain which Nature has infused in the first congelation of mercury, all metals having one origin and a common substance, as will be ultimately unveiled to those who become worthy of receiving it by application and assiduous study.

Q. What follows from this doctrine?
A. It follows that, although the seed is more perfect in gold, it may be extracted much more easily from another body than from gold itself, other bodies being more open, that is to say, less digested, and less restricted in their humidity.

Q. Give me an example taken from Nature.
A. Vulgar gold may be likened to a fruit which, having come to a perfect maturity, has been cut off from its tree, and though it contains a most perfect and well-digested seed, notwithstanding, should anyone set it in the ground, with a view to its multiplication, much time, trouble, and attention will be consumed in the development of its vegetative capabilities. On the other hand, if a cutting, or a root, be taken from the same tree, and similarly planted, in a short time, and with no trouble, it will spring up and produce much fruit.

Q. Is it necessary that an amateur of this science should understand the formation of metals in the bowels of the earth if he wishes to complete his work?
A. So indispensable is such a knowledge that should anyone fail, before all other studies, to apply himself to its attainment, and to imitate Nature point by point therein, he will never succeed in accomplishing anything but what is worthless.

Q. How, then, does Nature deposit metals in the bowels of the earth, and of what does she compose them?
A. Nature manufactures them all out of sulphur and mercury, and forms them by their double vapour.

Q. What do you mean by this double vapour, and how can metals be formed thereby?
A. In order to a complete understanding of this question, it must first be stated that mercurial vapour is united to sulphureous vapour in a cavernous place which contains a saline water, which serves as their matrix. Thus is formed, firstly, the Vitriol of Nature; secondly, by the commotion of

the elements, there is developed out of this Vitriol of Nature a new vapour, which is neither mercurial nor sulphureous, yet is allied to both these natures, and this, passing through places to which the grease of sulphur adheres, is joined therewith, and out of their union a glutinous substance is produced, otherwise, a formless mass, which is permeated by the vapour that fills these cavernous places. By this vapour, acting through the sulphur it contains, are produced the perfect metals, provided that the vapour and the locality are pure. If the locality and the vapour are impure, imperfect metals result. The terms perfection and imperfection have reference to various degrees of concoction.

Q. What is contained in this vapour?
A. A spirit of light and a spirit of fire, of the nature of the celestial bodies, which properly should be considered as the form of the universe.

Q. What does this vapour represent?
A. This vapour, thus impregnated by the universal spirit, represents, in a fairly complete way, the original Chaos, which contained all that was required for the original creation, that is, universal matter and universal form.

Q. And one cannot, notwithstanding, make use of vulgar mercury in the process?
A. No, because vulgar mercury, as already made plain, is devoid of external agent.

Q. Whence comes it that common mercury is without its external agent?
A. Because in the exaltation of the double vapour, the

commotion has been so great and searching, that the spirit, or agent, has evaporated, as occurs, with very close similarity, in the fusion of metals. The result is that the unique mercurial part is deprived of its masculine or sulphureous agent, and consequently can never be transmuted into gold by Nature.

Q. How many species of gold are distinguished by the Philosophers?
A. Three sorts :--Astral Gold, Elementary Gold, and Vulgar Gold.

Q. What is astral gold?
A. Astral Gold has its centre in the sun, which communicates it by its rays to all inferior beings. It is an igneous substance, which receives a continual emanation of solar corpuscles that penetrate all things sentient, vegetable, and mineral.

Q. What do you refer to under the term Elementary Gold?
A. This is the most pure and fixed portion of the elements, and of all that is composed of them. All sublunary beings included in the three kingdoms contain in their inmost centre a precious grain of this elementary gold.

Q. Give me some description of Vulgar Gold?
A. It is the most beautiful metal of our acquaintance, the best that Nature can produce, as perfect as it is unalterable in itself.

Q. Of what species of gold is the Stone of the Philosophers?
A. It is of the second species, as being the most pure portion of all the metallic elements after its purification, when it is termed living philosophical gold. A perfect equilibrium and equality of the four elements enter into the Physical Stone,

and four things are indispensable for the accomplishment of the work, namely, composition, allocation, mixture, and union, which, once performed according to the rules of art, will beget the lawful Son of the Sun, and the Phoenix which eternally rises out of its own ashes.

Q. What is actually the living gold of the Philosophers?
A. It is exclusively the fire of Mercury, or that igneous virtue, contained in the radical moisture, to which it has already communicated the fixity and the nature of the sulphur, whence it has emanated, the mercurial character of the whole substance of philosophical sulphur permitting it to be alternatively termed mercury.

Q. What other name is also given by the Philosophers to their living gold ?
A. They also term it their living sulphur, and their true fire; they recognize its existence in all bodies, and there is nothing that can subsist without it.

Q. Where must we look for our living gold, our living sulphur, and our true fire ?
A. In the house of Mercury.

Q. By what is this fire nourished?
A. By the air.

Q. Give me a comparative illustration of the power of this fire?
A. To exemplify the attraction of this interior fire, there is no better comparison than that which is derived from the thunderbolt, which originally is simply a dry, terrestrial

exhalation, united to a humid vapour. By exaltation, and by assuming the igneous nature, it acts on the humidity which is inherent to it; this it attracts to itself, transmutes it into its own nature, and then rapidly precipitates itself to the earth, where it is attracted by a fixed nature which is like unto its own.

Q. What should be done by the Philosopher after he has extracted his Mercury?
A. He should develop it from potentiality into activity.

Q. Cannot Nature perform this of herself?
A. No; because she stops short after the first sublimation, and out of the matter which is thus disposed do the metals engender.

Q. What do the Philosophers understand by their gold and silver?
A. The Philosophers apply to their Sulphur the name of Gold, and to their Mercury the name of Silver.

Q. Whence are they derived?
A. I have already stated that they are derived from a homogeneous body wherein they are found in great abundance, whence also Philosophers know how to extract both by an admirable, and entirely philosophical, process.

Q. When this operation has been duly performed, to what other point of the practice must they next apply themselves?
A. To the confection of the philosophical amalgam, which must be done with great care, but can only be accomplished after the preparation and sublimation of the Mercury.

Q. When should your matter be combined with the living gold?
A. During the period of amalgamation only, that is to say, Sulphur is introduced into it by means of the amalgamation, and thenceforth there is one substance; the process is shortened by the addition of Sulphur, while the tincture at the same time is augmented.

Q. What is contained in the centre of the radical moisture?
A. It contains and conceals Sulphur, which is covered with a hard rind.

Q. What must be done to apply it to the Great Work?
A. It must be drawn, out of its bonds with consummate skill, and by the method of putrefaction.

Q. Does Nature, in her work in the mines, possess a menstruum which is adapted to the dissolution and liberation of this sulphur?
A. No; because there is no local movement. Could Nature, unassisted, dissolve, putrefy, and purify the metallic body, she would herself provide us with !he Physical Stone, which is Sulphur exalted and increased in virtue.

Q. Can you elucidate this doctrine by an example?
A. By an enlargement of the previous comparison of a fruit, or a seed, which, in the first place, is put into the earth for its solution, and afterwards for its multiplication. Now, the Philosopher, who is in a position to discern what is good seed, extracts it from its centre, consigns it to its proper earth, when it has been well cured and prepared, and therein he rarefies it

in such a manner that its prolific virtue is increased and indefinitely multiplied.

Q. In what does the whole secret of the seed consist?
A. In the true knowledge of its proper earth.

Q. What do you understand by the seed in the work Of the Philosophers?
A. I understand the interior heat, or the specific spirit, which is enclosed in the humid radical, which, in other words, is the middle substance of living silver, the proper sperm of metals, which contains its own seed.

Q. How do you set free the sulphur from its bonds?
A. By putrefaction.

Q. What is the earth of minerals?
A. It is their proper menstruum.

Q. What pains must be taken by the Philosopher to extract that part which he requires?
A. He must take great pains to eliminate the fetid vapours and impure sulphurs, after which the seed must be injected.

Q. By what indication may the Artist be assured that he is in the right road at the beginning of his work?
A. When he finds that the dissolvent and the thing dissolved are converted into one form and one matter at the period of dissolution.

Q. How many solutions do you count in the Philosophic Work?
A. There are three. The first solution is that which reduces the

crude and metallic body into its elements of sulphur and of living silver; the second is that of the physical body, and the third is the solution of the mineral earth.

Q. How is the metallic body reduced by the first solution into mercury, and then into sulphur?
A. By the secret artificial fire, which is the Burning Star.

Q. How is this operation performed?
A. By extracting from the subject, in the first place, the mercury or vapour of the elements, and, after purification, by using it to liberate the sulphur from its bonds, by corruption, of which blackness is the indication.

Q. How is the second solution performed?
A. When the physical body is resolved into the two substances previously mentioned, and has acquired the celestial nature.

Q. What is the name which is applied by Philosophers to the Matter during this period?
A, It is called their Physical Chaos, and it is, in fact, the true First Matter, a name which can hardly be applied before the conjunction of the male--which is sulphur--with the female--which is silver.

Q. To what does the third solution refer?
A. It is the humectation of the mineral earth and it is closely bound up with multiplication.

Q. What fire must be made use of in our work?
A. That fire which is used by Nature.

Q. What is the potency of this fire?
A. It dissolves everything that is in the world, because it is the principle of all dissolution and corruption.

Q. Why is it also termed Mercury?
A. Because it is in its nature aerial, and a most subtle vapour, which partakes at the same time of sulphur, whence it has contracted some contamination.

Q. Where is this fire concealed?
A. It is concealed in the subject of art.

Q. Who is it that is familiar with, and can produce, this fire?
A. It is known to the wise, who can both produce it and purify it.

Q. What is the essential potency and characteristic of this fire?
A. It is excessively dry, and is continually in motion; it seeks only to disintegrate and to educe things from potentiality into actuality; it is that, in a word, which coming upon solid places in mines, circulates in a vaporous form upon the matter, and dissolves it.

Q. How may this fire be most easily distinguished?
A. By the sulphureous excrements in which it is enveloped, and by the saline environment with which it is clothed.

Q. What must be added to this fire so as to accentuate its capacity for incineration in the feminine species?
A. On account of its extreme dryness it requires to be moistened.

Q. How many philosophical fires do you enumerate?
A. There are in all three--the natural, the unnatural, and the contra-natural.

Q. Explain to me these three species of fires.
A. The natural fire is the masculine fire, or the chief agent; the unnatural is the feminine, which is the dissolvent of Nature, nourishing a white smoke, and assuming that form. This smoke is quickly dissipated, unless much care be exercised, and it is almost incombustible, though by philosophical sublimation it becomes corporeal and resplendent. The contra-natural fire is that which disintegrates compounds and has the power to unbind what has' been bound very closely by Nature.

Q. Where is our matter to be found?
A. It is to be found everywhere, but it must specially be sought in metallic nature, where it is more easily available than elsewhere.

Q. What kind must be preferred before all others?
A. The most mature, the most appropriate, and the easiest; but care, before all things, must be taken that the metallic essence shall be present, not only potentially but in actuality, and that there is, moreover, a metallic splendour.

Q. Is everything contained in this subject?
A. Yes; but Nature, at the same time, must be assisted, so that the work may be perfected and hastened, and this by the means which are familiar to the higher grades of experiment.

Q. Is this subject exceedingly precious?
A. It is vile, and originally is without native elegance; should anyone say that it is saleable, it is the species to which they refer, but, fundamentally, it is not saleable, because it is useful in our work alone.

Q. What does our Matter contain?
A. It contains Salt, Sulphur, and Mercury.

Q. What operation is it most important to be able to perform?
A. The successive extraction of the Salt, Sulphur, and Mercury.

Q. How is that done?
A. By sole and perfect sublimation.

Q. What is in the first place extracted?
A. Mercury in the form of a white smoke.

Q. What follows?
A. Igneous water, or Sulphur.

Q. What then?
A. Dissolution with purified salt, in the first place volatilising that which is fixed, and afterwards fixing that which is volatile into a precious earth, which is the Vase of the Philosophers, and is wholly perfect.

Q. When must the Philosopher begin his enterprise?
A. At the moment of daybreak, for his energy must never be relaxed.

Q. When may he take his rest?
A. When the work has come to its perfection.

Q. At what hour is the end of the work ?
A. High noon, that is to say, the moment when the Sun is in its fullest power, and the Son of the Day-Star in its most brilliant splendour.

Q. What is the pass-word of Magnesia?
A. You know whether I can or should answer:--I reserve my speech.

Q. Give me the greeting of the Philosophers.
A. Begin ; I will reply to you.

Q. Are you an apprentice Philosopher?
A. My friends, and the wise, know me.

Q. What is the age of a Philosopher ?
A. From the moment of his researches to that of his discoveries, the Philosopher does not age.

www.ingramcontent.com/pod-product-compliance
Lightning Source LLC
LaVergne TN
LVHW041502070426
835507LV00009B/771